WONDERWISE™

Trucks

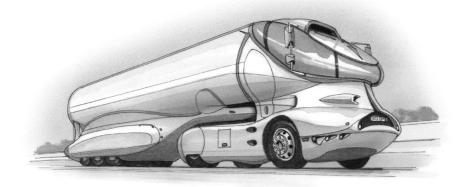

Published by Smart Apple Media,
an imprint of Black Rabbit Books
P.O. Box 3263, Mankato, Minnesota 56002
www.blackrabbitbooks.com

Published by arrangement with
The Salariya Book Company Ltd

Cataloging-in-Publication Data is available
from the Library of Congress

Printed in the United States
At Corporate Graphics,
North Mankato, Minnesota

9 8 7 6 5 4 3 2 1

ISBN: 978-1-62588-363-6

Illustrators: Mark Bergin
Nick Hewetson
Gerald Wood
David Antram
Tony Townsend

WONDERWISE™

Trucks

KEVIN INGRAM

Smart Apple Media

CONTENTS

INTRODUCTION

Trucks rumble down our roads both day and night. They have been given an important job to do, transporting goods from one end of the country to the other—from ports to factories, from factories to stores, and from stores to our homes. Since their first appearance more than 100 years ago, trucks have changed their engines and design, and now do much more than deliver goods. They work on building sites, keep our streets clean, and provide emergency services at moments of life and death.

WHAT IS A TRUCK?

A liquid load, such as milk, petrol, or wine is carried in a long tube-shaped tank. Trucks like these are called tankers.

A truck is a motor vehicle that carries goods from one place to another. It can be anything from a small pick-up truck to a thundering juggernaut. A truck's size, weight, and design all depend on the job it does—from carrying groceries to transporting rock from a quarry.

Flatbed trailer

◀ Trucks are used to shift loads around the farm. These flatbed trailers are stacked with hay.

▼ We see delivery trucks every day of the year, transporting goods all over the country. They manage to get to stores in the most remote places.

Delivery truck

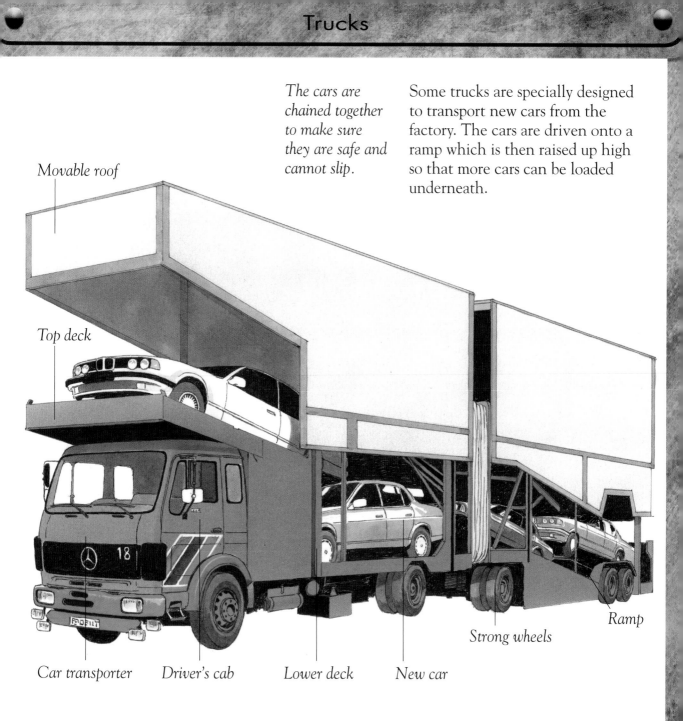

The cars are chained together to make sure they are safe and cannot slip.

Some trucks are specially designed to transport new cars from the factory. The cars are driven onto a ramp which is then raised up high so that more cars can be loaded underneath.

Movable roof

Top deck

Car transporter   Driver's cab   Lower deck   New car   Strong wheels   Ramp

A logging truck

◀ A logging truck is both heavy and powerful. It carries tree trunks down from forest plantations.

▲ Some transporters have a movable roof, which drops down over the cars. This protects them on the way to the salesroom.

EARLY TRUCKS

▲ *This German van had a diesel engine. Diesel engines use less fuel than gasoline engines and are cheaper to run.*

bout 200 years ago, the only way to travel or carry goods was behind a gently plodding horse. In the early 1800s, carriages began to appear that were powered by steam engines. These heavy, smoky vehicles were never very popular. As soon as gasoline engines were invented, bringing in faster, lighter, vehicles, the old steam carriages began to disappear.

▼ *This 16-seat steam coach was built in 1830. It traveled over 12 mph (20 kph) but had no brakes. The steam engine would cool off and the coach would slow down.*

▲ In the early 1900s, most goods were transported by rail. To deliver goods to the doorstep, the railroad company still relied on horse and cart.

Ox-drawn wagon

▲ The American pioneer's ox-drawn wagon was a distant ancestor of today's truck.

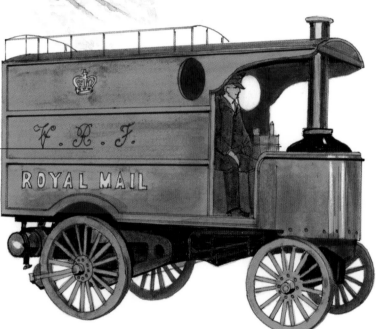

◄ *Towards the end of the 1800s, many delivery trucks still ran on steam, like this old mail van.*

ROYAL MAIL

▼ The French engineer, Nicolas Cugnot, invented the first steam carriage in 1769. It was used by the army to pull heavy cannon.

Cugnot's steam carriage

THE FIRST TRUCKS

The first trucks replaced horse-drawn carriages as a way for people to get around. But they were soon used as ambulances, fire trucks, road sweepers, and even funeral carriages. Trucks also delivered goods, of course—not only in towns, but from one end of the country to another.

To keep up with the growing number of trucks, better roads were built, and these helped to cut down journey times. But trains still delivered most goods—and did so until the late 1950s.

▲ *The development of the horseless carriage began in the mid-1800s.*

▲ *London's first gasoline-engine buses appeared around 1900.*

Chicago
Cleveland
Detroit
Burton-Dixie Co
NEW YORK

◀ *Long-distance trucks drivers slept in a bed on top of the cab.*

▶ To avoid punctures, trucks had extra wheels and axles to spread the weight.

Diesel truck

By the 1930s, steam engines were being replaced by new diesel trucks. Diesel oil was cheap and went a very long way.

Studded wheels

▼ *This handsome six-wheeled delivery truck belonged to a brewery in Canada during the 1940s.*

▲ *This snowplow was built in about 1920. It was a truck with studded wheels that stopped it getting stuck in snow.*

▶ New air-filled tires gave drivers a more comfortable ride.

Air-filled tires.

AT THE FAIRGROUND

Traveling showpeople have always had to move heavy equipment from one fairground to another. In the late 1800s, steam-powered traction engines appeared. These traction engines could not only pull the heavy wagons, but could generate the power to drive the rides. Traction engines were strong and reliable, and they looked good too. Many of them were decorated with gleaming brass and colorful paintwork. They caused great excitement when they pulled into town.

▶ *These marvelous traction engines were still being used in the 1950s.*

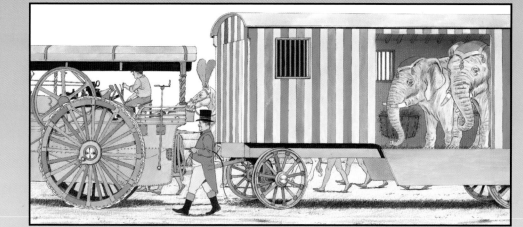

RECORD BREAKERS

Monster trucks like Bigfoot compete at truck events. They try to outdo each other in events including doing wheelies and climbing over obstacles.

The fastest, the slowest, the biggest, the smallest—the world of trucks has its own record breakers. These are not trucks that you see every day on roads. You may not have seen any of them before. These record breakers have all been specially designed to do a particular job in a particular place—that is what makes them remarkable.

Terex Titan

▼ The fastest truck in the world is called Shockwave. Instead of the usual diesel engine, it has three jet engines, which are normally used on a plane. No wonder it can move at over 370 mph (600 kph).

Shockwave

Besch Racer

Motorcraft
Fast-cote
TWISTA SIMPSON

The Terex Titan was the world's biggest dump truck for 25 years. Its driver could just reach the bottom ring of the ladder up to the cab.

▼ This truck moves up and down the rows of a Brazilian coffee plantation, picking ripe fruits from the coffee plants. It was the first truck in the world to do this job successfully.

▼ The flattest trucks are the "tugs" that tow planes around an airport. They are low and flat so that they can zip under a plane's wings.

▼ This little dumper is more like a wheelbarrow than a truck. It carries about 1.6 U.S. tons (1.5 metric tons) and must be one of the smallest trucks in the world.

Airport tug

MODERN TRUCKS

Trucks have come a long way from the slow, drafty vehicles they once were. Today's supertrucks are comfortable and reliable, and can cruise at high speed for many hours. A truck carries such heavy loads that its chassis has to be strong. All this extra weight needs a more powerful engine to pull it—about four times more powerful than a car's—and equally powerful brakes.

▼ *Scania T500 LA 4X2 HNA. This modern truck has a 15.6 liter engine.*

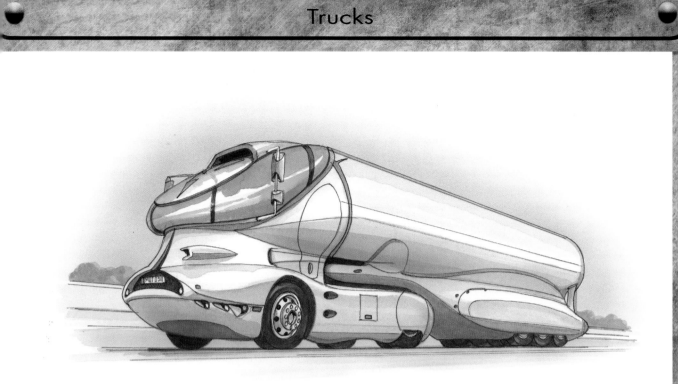

▲ Designed by Luigi Colani this aerodynamic truck is inspired by nature. Colani's aim was to design a streamline truck that consumed less fuel.

▼ The Renault T series won the International Truck of the Year competition in 2015. The T Series is used by Formula 1 teams to transport race cars.

TRUCKS AROUND THE WORLD

Trucks are one of the most successful forms of road transport. They are so strong and tough that they can reach small villages that are many days' drive away from the nearest railroad. This is why trucks are now used in every part of the world. The design of the truck, and the job it does, will often change from one place to another— whether it is in the forests of Canada, the grasslands of Africa, or the burning Australian outback.

Logging truck

▲ The forests of Canada produce many tons of lumber. The giant logs are carried to the sawmill on huge trucks.

▶ In Africa, safari trucks are a safe way to look for the animals. They provide a useful viewing platform, too.

Safari truck

▼ Australian road trains transport goods in places where there are no railways. The tractor pulls three or more trailers.

Road train

◄ *Drivers decorate their buses with special designs and messages that may bring them luck on the road.*

A bus in Pakistan

▲ Buses in Pakistan are heavy trucks that can cope with the hills.

► *This Swedish truck is really a police car. It visits schools with information about road safety.*

19

FIRE TRUCKS

A fire truck races along the street with its siren blaring as soon as a fire is reported. Fire trucks are fast-moving trucks that carry a lot of equipment—tools, ladders, lights, oxygen tanks, and so on.

Some of them even carry a large water tank, which pumps out water with a terrific force.

▶ A long boom carries fire-fighters high into the air, so that they can rescue people from the top of the building.

Boom

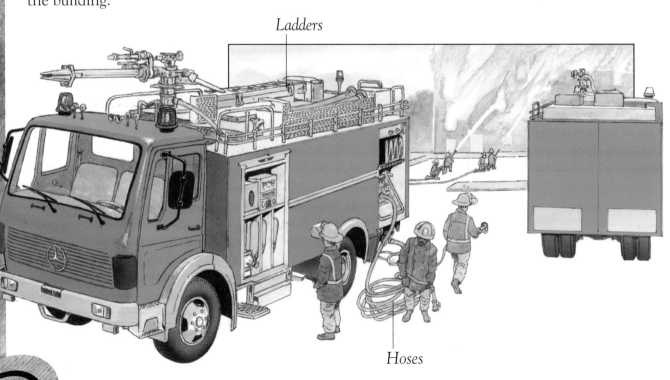

Ladders

Hoses

Simba

▲ At an airport fire, the Simba fire truck sprays foam over a burning plane.

Siren

Light

Exhaust

Storage compartment

▲ This fire engine belongs to the American Fire Department.

▲ Fire trucks have to react quickly. They leave within a number of minutes of a call, and reach speeds of 100 mph (160 kph).

AT THE BUILDING SITE

Crane

The cement truck delivers ready-made concrete to the building site. It is mixed inside the drum as the truck move along.

▶ A mobile crane is a truck with a crane on its back. It has "legs" to keep the truck steady as the crane is raised.

Truck transporter

Some trucks are too big to go on the roads. They are brought to the site on the back of huge transporters.

MAN

STGO
CAT 3

22

▶ Dump trucks deliver sand, gravel, and cement. Each truck can carry a load that is twice its own weight.

▼ Dump trucks are easy to unload. Their body tips back until the load slides out in a heap on the ground.

Trucks do much of the heavy work at a building site. As trenches and holes are dug, hard-working dump trucks carry away the soil and rubble. When building work begins, a fleet of trucks speed to and fro, bringing load after load of building materials.

Other trucks, such as the cement mixer or crane truck, carry special equipment that is used at the building site itself.

Cement truck

Dump truck

Concrete is mixed inside the drum.

HEAVY LOADS

Every truck is designed to carry a load. Most loads are heavy, but some are truly enormous, weighing hundreds of tons. A weight like this would snap the axles of lighter vehicles, but the strongest trucks have dozens of axles, and as many as fifty wheels. These help to spread the weight over the whole truck.

Big trucks drive slowly, and take up a lot of room on the road. They often have a police escort, which helps to warn other drivers.

Salt

Trailer

Cab

Dart truck at work in a Mexican salt mine.

▲ The Dart truck is used in Mexico to carry salt. It is massive, and can carry a load of over 390 U.S. tons (350 metric tons) on its journey from the salt mine to the port.

▶ The first U.S. space shuttle was carried to the launch pad on a huge truck called the crawler. It had caterpillar tracks instead of tires.

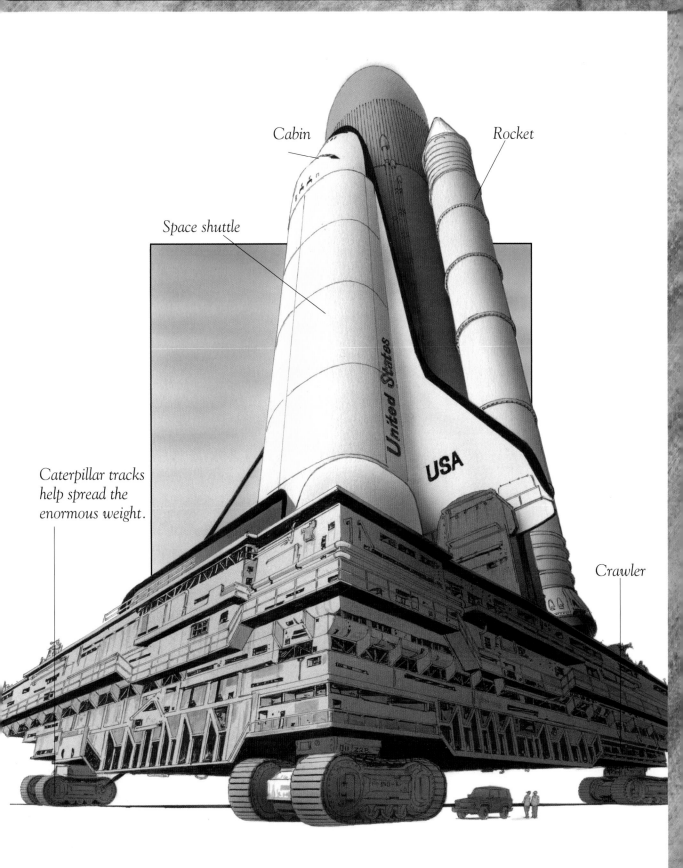

Cabin

Rocket

Space shuttle

Caterpillar tracks
help spread the
enormous weight.

United States

USA

Crawler

AMBULANCES

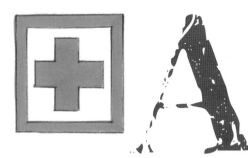

Ambulances are fast, powerful trucks that are specially built to deal with emergencies. Every day, trained ambulance crews rush to sick and injured people, give emergency treatment, and then rush them back to hospital. Ambulances give a smooth, comfortable ride, sparing their passengers any painful bumps. The equipment stored on board may help to keep some patients alive until they can have their full medical care.

▶ A wailing siren and flashing light warn other road users to get out of the way.

It is important to get to the scene of an accident quickly. Paramedics are trained to drive fast but safely.

▼ *This unusual vehicle was used during World War One. It was a bulletproof stretcher-on-wheels that carried wounded soldiers to safety.*

▲ *In the early 1900s, accidents doubled because of the new motor car. An ambulance service was started up with vehicles like this.*

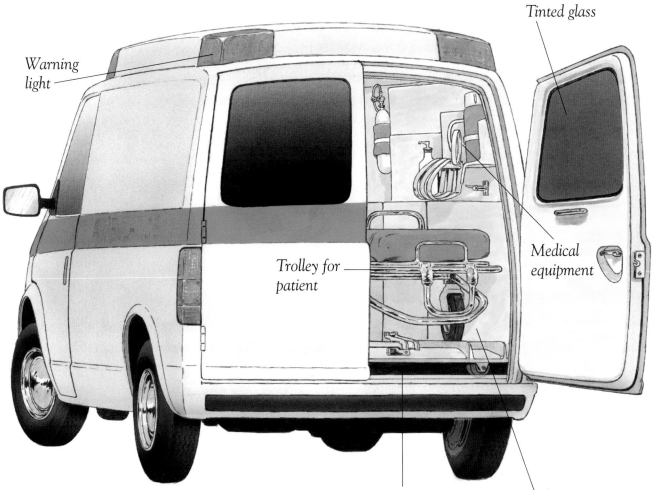

Warning
light

Tinted glass

Medical
equipment

Trolley for
patient

▲ The modern ambulance has
a radio so that the crew can tell
doctors at the hosptial about
the patient.

*Unfolding steps and wide-opening
doors make it easier for the crew to
carry patients into the ambulance.*

*There is room for
passengers, too.*

*War ambulance
1914–1918*

FUTURE AND CONCEPT TRUCKS

Trucks of the future may be self-driving, more fuel-efficient, and reach speeds of up to 50 mph (80 kph).

▲ *The Renault Radiance has been descibed as a "dream truck." Equipped with cameras instead of mirrors, a convertible sofa bed, and glass roof.*

▲ *The Mercedes Future Truck 2025 will be a self-driving long-distance truck. With a range of technological advancements such as radar sensors and a camera scan.*

▶*MAN (a German engineering company) have designed a new Concept S truck, which has the load volume of a conventional truck without the large fuel consumption.*

◄ Morita's Forest Fire Fighting Concept Car has been awarded the 2011 IDEA Gold Award for its innovative design.

▼ The Scania Concept Truck is an eco-friendly and economical truck designed by Adam Palethorpe.

▶ This futuristic truck from Mercedes-Benz will be self-driving as well as having a blind spot assist and stereo camera.

USEFUL WORDS

Axle Metal rod with wheels on each end. Wheels turn on the axle.

Caterpillar tracks Chains of metal plates, which are used on wheels instead of tires to spread the weight of the truck, and give grip on rough, muddy ground.

Chassis The body and working parts of a truck are built onto the chassis. It is a strong framework.

Diesel engine Type of engine used in most trucks. It burns a thick, heavy fuel called diesel, which is made from oil.

Gear Machinery inside a truck that allows the driver to control the power of the engine and the speed of the vehicle.

Generate To make or produce.

Soundproofing A way of keeping noise out of the cab—by padding for example.

Tanker Truck that is specially built to carry a liquid load.

Traction engine Heavy, steam-powered road vehicle that was once used to pull heavy loads and generate power.

Traction unit Front of an articulated truck. Contains the engine and the driver's cab.

Trailer unit The part of an articulated truck that carries the load, and is pulled by the tractor.

TIMELINE

c. 3500 Wheels are used for making pottery in Sumeria for the first time; wheels are used on wagons and carts about the same time.

c. 1550 The first wooden tracks for building mine and quarry trucks appear.

c. 1650 There are faster stage coaches in England.

1700 Plate-glass windows are fitted in coaches.

1769 French engineer, Nicolas Cugnot, invents the first steam carriage.

1787 Collinge's self-oiling axle for coaches is invented.

1844 Wells Fargo express mail coach service starts in the U.S. to serve the Western settlements.

c. 1990 London's first gasoline-engine buses appear.

c. 1930 Steam engines are being replaced by new diesel trucks.

1973 The Terex Titan is assembled in Canada. At the time it was the biggest dump truck ever made.

2011 The Morita Forest Fire Fighting Concept Car wins the IDEA Gold Award.

2015 The Renault T series wins International Truck of the Year.

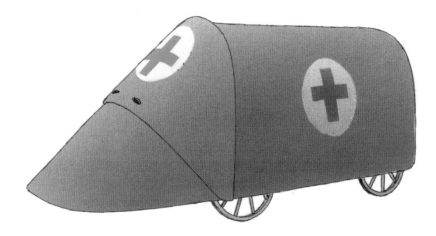

INDEX

A

airport 15, 21
ambulance 10, 26–27
axle 11, 24

B

building site 5, 22, 23
bus 10, 19

C

cab 7, 10, 15, 24
caterpillar tracks 24, 25
chassis 16
Colani, Luigi 17
crane truck 23
crawler 24, 25
Cugnot, Nicolas 9

D

Dart truck 24
delivery truck 6, 9, 11
diesel engine 8, 14
driver 7, 10, 11, 15, 19, 24

dump truck 15, 23

F

fairground truck 12–13
fire truck 10, 20–21

H

horse drawn vehicle 8, 9, 10

L

loads 6, 16, 24–25
logging truck 7, 18

M

MAN 28
Mercedes-Benz 28, 29
Morita 29

P

Palethorpe, Adam 29

R

railroad 9, 18, 19

Renault 17, 28
road trains 19

S

safari truck 18
Scania 16, 29
Shockwave 14
Simba 21
snowplow 11
steam engine 8, 11
supertrucks 16

T

tanker 6
tire 11, 24
Terex Titan 14, 15
traction engine 12, 13
trailer 6, 19, 24
transporter 7, 22
tug 15

W

wheel 7, 11, 15, 24, 26